Solo·Duet·Trio

Selected Themes from the Motion Picture

Harry Potter

and the
Sorcerer's Stone

Music by
JOHN WILLIAMS

Arranged by
VICTOR LÓPEZ

Contents

Flute (0645B)
Clarinet (0646B)
Alto Sax (0647B)
Tenor Sax (0648B)
Trumpet (0649B)
Horn (0650B)
Trombone (0651B)

D1572781

Album Cover Artwork © 2001 Warner Bros.

HEDWIG'S THEME

TROMBONE
(Baritone, Bassoon, Tuba)

Music by **JOHN WILLIAMS**
Arranged by VICTOR LÓPEZ

Misterioso ♩ = 152

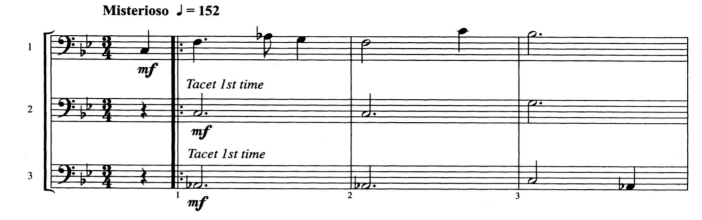

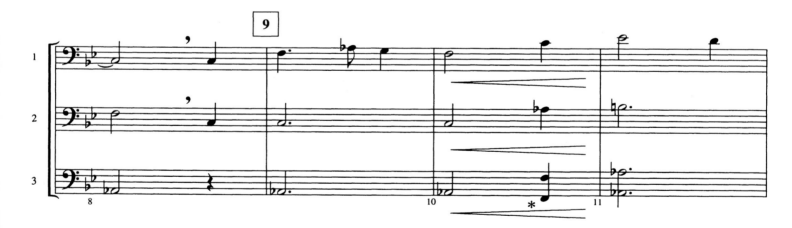

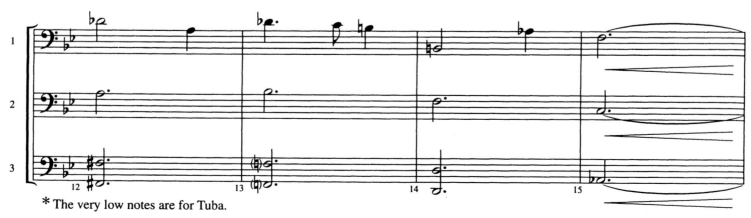

* The very low notes are for Tuba.

3

DIAGON ALLEY

Music by **JOHN WILLIAMS**
Arranged by VICTOR LÓPEZ

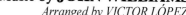

* Try to play the sixteenth notes (stems down); if they are too hard, play eighth notes (stems up).

HOGWARTS FOREVER

Music by **JOHN WILLIAMS**
Arranged by VICTOR LÓPEZ

Stately and nobly ♩ = 88

*Gb = F#.

NIMBUS 2000

Music by **JOHN WILLIAMS**
Arranged by VICTOR LÓPEZ

*Cb = B♮; Gb = F♯.

CAST A CHRISTMAS SPELL

Music and Lyrics by **JOHN WILLIAMS**
Arranged by VICTOR LÓPEZ

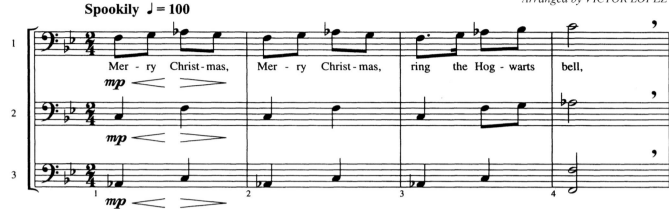

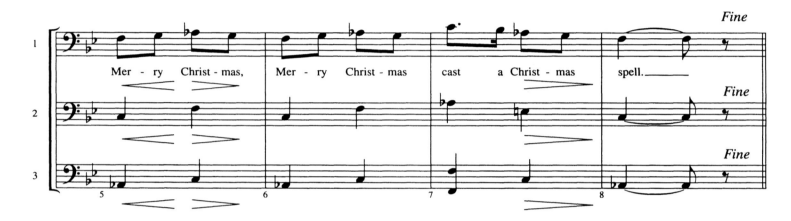

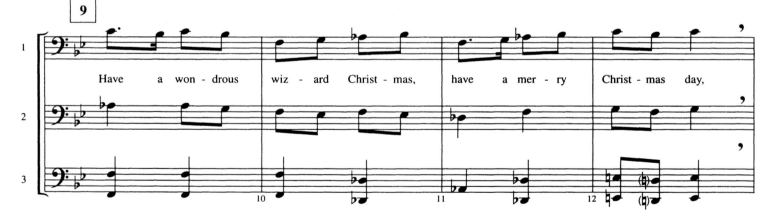

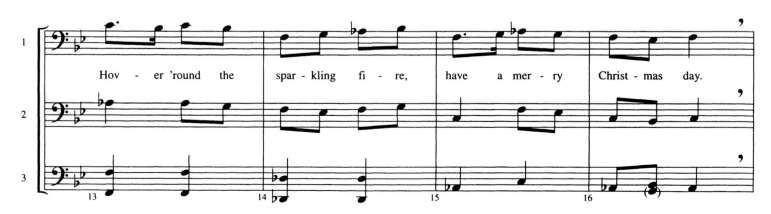

HARRY'S WONDROUS WORLD

Music by **JOHN WILLIAMS**
Arranged by VICTOR LÓPEZ

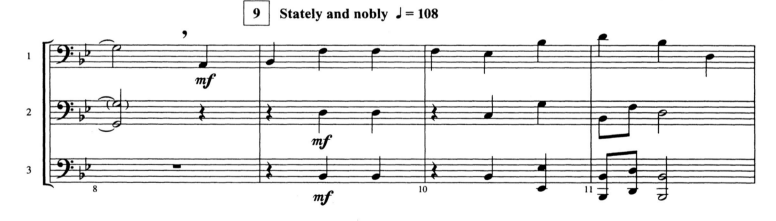

* Gb = F#; Cb = B♮; Fb = E♮.

0651B

PARTS OF A TROMBONE AND POSITION CHART

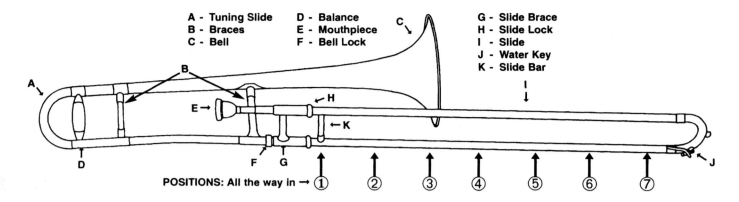

How To Read The Chart

The number of the position for each note is given in the chart below. See the picture above for the location of the slide bar for each position. When two enharmonic tones are given on the chart (F# and G♭ as an example), they sound the same and are played with the same position. Alternate positions are shown underneath for trombones with a trigger (T=thumb trigger).

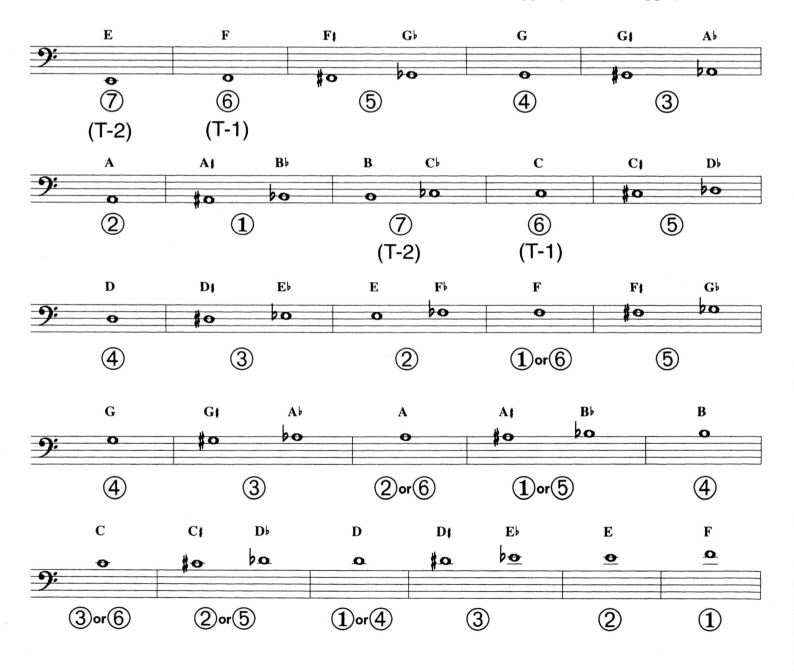